Do Witches Exist?

**Other titles in the *Do They Exist?*
series include:**

Do They Exist?

Do Witches Exist?

Patricia D. Netzley

ReferencePoint
Press®

San Diego, CA

© 2016 ReferencePoint Press, Inc.
Printed in the United States

For more information, contact:
ReferencePoint Press, Inc.
PO Box 27779
San Diego, CA 92198
www.ReferencePointPress.com

LIBRARY OF CONGRESS CATALOGING-IN-PUBLICATION DATA

Netzley, Patricia D.
  Do witches exist? / by Patricia D. Netzley.
      pages cm. -- (Do they exist?)
  Includes bibliographical references and index.
  Audience: Grade 9 to 12.
  ISBN-13: 978-1-60152-862-9 (hardback)
  ISBN-10: 1-60152-862-0 (hardback)
  1. Witches--Juvenile literature. I. Title.
BF1566.N47 2016
133.4'3--dc23

                                                                    2015005633

Contents

Introduction

Witches and Witchcraft

When people think of witches, many envision a hag with a warty nose and a pointy black hat, perhaps accompanied by a bubbling cauldron, a broom, and a black cat. This image has been cultivated over time in literature and movies and through traditions like Halloween. But unlike zombies and werewolves, which have been similarly exploited, witches are not products of the imagination. They are real people who have been part of the fabric of many cultures throughout history. This means that their existence is not in question. However, whether they can actually create magic through their practice of witchcraft has long been a matter of controversy.

Cunning Folk

Among the earliest practitioners of witchcraft were folk healers, known in some parts of the world as wise or cunning folk. (The word cunning comes from kenning, old English for "knowing" or "wise.") Such people had knowledge of traditional or folk medicine that had been passed down from their ancestors, and some of their remedies involved the use of charms or words believed to be magic. For example, in Scandinavia in medieval times, de kloka (meaning "the wise ones") used magic rhymes as part of attempts to heal people or to ensure the safe delivery of a child. In Denmark the kloga folk ("wise folk") typically carried a book that contained formulas for creating healing charms. Many of these charms were intended to ease pain. For example, to treat a toothache, the sufferer or healer would write certain words on a piece of paper, which would be placed onto the aching tooth before bed; in the morning, the sufferer would spit the paper into the hearth fire.

In centuries past, a practitioner of witchcraft whose magic seemed to work—whether in improving health or in bringing about some other desirable result—often had enhanced stature in a community. Conversely, when a practitioner's magic failed to work, people typically doubted the skills of the healer or witch rather than the power of magic. This was largely because prior to modern times, most people did not question that magic was real. Instead, they questioned the skills of the practitioner.

Causing Harm

This conviction that witches had magic powers sometimes led to accusations of witchcraft being used to cause harm. For example, if a witch was engaged in a dispute with a neighbor and that neighbor died unexpectedly or under inexplicable circumstances, people often suspected that the witch had caused the death via an evil spell. The prospect that a witch might be practicing evil magic, commonly known as black magic, often created fear in a community. Sometimes this fear would lead villagers to drive suspected or professed witches away, but in some places it was more common that the witch would be put to death.

During the thirteenth through seventeenth centuries, witch persecution in Europe often stemmed from religious beliefs as well because members of the dominant religion, Catholicism, believed that witchcraft was anti-Christian. They accused witches of consorting with Christ's enemy, Satan, and using their witchcraft for evil purposes. It is unknown how many witch executions took place during this time. Whereas some experts say tens of thousands, others say well over a hundred thousand. But in any case, although people might doubt whether a particular condemned person really did have magic powers, their belief that magic was real remained high.

This postcard from the early 1900s illustrates a popular conception of wicked witches. The witch is depicted as an older woman wearing antiquated clothing that includes a pointed hat. She flies through the air on a broomstick with her familiar, a black cat.

Modern Witches

Today this sentiment is not nearly as common. According to a 2013 Harris poll, 54 percent of Americans do not believe that witches have magic powers. Even so, polls have found that teenagers maintain an interest in witchcraft. Roughly three-fourths of teens have engaged in some sort of activity related to witchcraft, such as reading a book on how to practice witchcraft or trying to cast a magic spell, mix a magic potion, or create a magic amulet. Moreover, people in various countries throughout the world still identify themselves as witches.

Most also see themselves as members of a specific witchcraft tradition, a collection of rituals and other activities passed on to them by others. These traditions guide the witchcraft practitioner in how to create magic. For example, in some traditions the practitioner calls upon certain deities or magical beings while performing rituals as part of elaborate ceremonies. This is known as ceremonial magic. In other traditions the practitioner calls upon the magical forces of nature. This is known as natural magic. A witch's tradition also influences his or her reliance on the use of herbs, candles, potions, amulets, and divination tools in performing witchcraft.

Witchcraft Traditions

Many witchcraft traditions are based on magic and worship practices from ancient times. For example, the Pictish tradition draws on the polytheistic nature-based rituals of the Picts, a Celtic people who lived in what is now eastern and northern Scotland during the late Iron Age and early medieval periods. The Druidic tradition draws on what little is known about practices of the ancient Druids, who were priests among the Celtic peoples of Gaul, Britain, and Ireland.

Other witchcraft traditions have been created by individuals. For example, in the 1950s an occultist (a scholar of magic) in England, Gerald Gardner, developed the Gardnerian tradition, which he later said drew from the pagan beliefs of a coven to which he once belonged. (A coven is a group of witches that meets regularly.) In the 1960s occultist Alex Sanders used Gardnerian rituals and beliefs as the foundation for his own tradition, the Alexandrian tradition, although he placed more of an emphasis on ceremonial magic than Gardner did. Another prominent witchcraft tradition, Seax-Wicca, was started by occultist Raymond Buckland in 1973 based on the religious and magical practices of the Saxons, a Germanic people who conquered England during the fifth century.

Most witches who identify themselves as belonging to a tradition meet in groups. Witches who practice alone typically either follow no tradition, in which case they are called solitary witches, or practice magic in ways drawn from a variety of traditions, in which case they are called eclectic witches.

Wicca

Regardless of their tradition, many modern witches also practice a form of Wicca, which has been called both a pagan religion and a witchcraft religion. In fact, so many witches consider themselves Wiccans that some people consider the words *Wicca* and *witchcraft* to be interchangeable. However, this is not the case. As Patti Wigington, an expert on Wicca, notes, "Wicca and witchcraft are not synonymous. One can be a witch without being Wiccan. Wicca itself is a specific religion. Those who follow it . . . honor the deities of their particular tradition of Wicca."[1]

By the same token, people of other religions can be witches. As Christian witch Zöe Grace explains, "Witchcraft is a practice. You can be a witch and be ANY religion. Just like you can practice Yoga and be any religion. Not all Yogis [yoga practitioners] are Hindu."[2]

Not Caricatures

In other words, in modern times anyone can be a witch. But such people are not the caricatured witches of fairy tales and popular entertainment. Most are ordinary individuals who just happen to practice some form of witchcraft. Ms. Ravenhawk, a Wiccan priestess who helped found the Wiccan Family Temple Academy of Pagan Studies in New York, says that those who study witchcraft at her school "are people with normal lives and normal jobs," although "not all of them are willing to identify themselves and talk about it for fear of what other people might think, especially in the workplace."[3]

> "Witchcraft is a practice. You can be a witch and be ANY religion."[2]
>
> —Christian witch Zöe Grace.

Indeed, even today witches can be ostracized for practicing witchcraft, although in most countries they no longer have to worry that they might be put to death for doing so. Sometimes they are ridiculed for believing in magic. Other times they are excluded from groups because they are thought to be evil. Some people still believe that witches associate with Satan, despite the fact that most witches do not believe in Satan. One of the students at Ravenhawk's school, a woman who goes by the name Ms. Collins, reports having to deal with such misperceptions, saying,

My mother knows that I am a Wiccan witch, but most of my family does not. People like my grandmother who are not as open-minded and do not believe in diversity, they just wouldn't understand, but this is not an evil religion. We do not worship the devil—we do not even believe in the devil. This is about connecting with the natural forces to advance yourself spiritually.[4]

Many witches feel compelled to hide their beliefs and practices from nonwitches, so it is impossible to know just how many witches exist. But because the Internet offers anonymity, witches are increasingly talking about their practices online, thereby providing outsiders with insights into what witchcraft really entails. This, in turn, is attracting more people to the magical arts, even though no one has yet been able to prove that real magic exists.

Chapter 1

What Is Witchcraft?

"The magic of most early nations aimed at causing the transference of power from a supernatural being to man, whereby he was to be enabled to obtain superhuman results and to become for a time as mighty as the original possessor of the power."

—English Egyptologist E.A. Wallis Budge.

E.A. Wallis Budge, *Egyptian Magic,* Sacred Texts. www.sacred-texts.com.

"Magic is the art and science of causing change to occur in conformity with will."

—Famed occultist Aleister Crowley.

Aleister Crowley, *Magic in Theory and Practice: Introduction and Theorems,* Sacred Texts. www.sacred-texts.com.

Quite simply, witchcraft is the practice of magic—not the illusions that stage magicians create, but rather a power that allows someone to control the natural world through supernatural or paranormal means. Many witches use the term *magick* to differentiate the magic of witchcraft from stage magic. Witches generally use magic words, magic actions, magic rituals, and magic objects in their work. In some combination, these are believed to allow them to manipulate unseen forces in accordance with their will so that they might achieve a desired result, such as the acquisition of personal wealth or the protection of a person, place, or thing.

Ceremonial Magic

There are two basic approaches to the practice of magic: ceremonial magic and folk magic. Ceremonial magic, or high magic, takes place as part of ceremonies that feature complicated rituals requiring the practitioner to say and do specific things in specific ways. Folk magic, or low magic, might involve rituals as well, but they are simple, not part of any ceremony, and can be performed in various ways.

Because ceremonial magic is complex, knowledge of its rituals has traditionally been passed down through books. Consequently, in centuries past, when many people were illiterate, it was practiced only by the highborn and well educated. In fact, even today its complexity makes it inaccessible to many people. Astrologer Estelle Daniels explains.

> Unfortunately much of Ceremonial Magick is quite formula oriented, complicated and demands a thorough knowledge of astrology . . . and other disciplines, and by the way a knowledge of Hebrew would be very useful also [because many of its practices are drawn from Jewish mysticism]. This is quite a lot, and for the average person, it is more than they are willing to take on, just to see if that system is right for them.[5]

Ceremonial magic requires special tools and preparations as well. For example, rituals are typically conducted within a magic circle, a space that has been ritually cleansed and outlined. In addition, rituals involve the summoning of spirits or forces, such as the elemental spirits of earth, air, fire, and water.

Ceremonial magic also relies on associations—or, as experts in magic call them, correspondences—between certain ideas and objects. For example, a ritual or spell drawing upon the power of the wind would involve correspondences to the element air. These include the color blue, the direction east, and ritual tools such as wands (because they are made from tree branches that once swayed in the wind). The element air also corresponds to certain gemstones, plants, and astrological signs and to various aspects of mental energy, such as creativity and reason.

Folk Magic

In contrast, folk magic is straightforward and concerns itself with practical matters, such as healing a wound, attracting a lover, finding a lost object, or increasing a harvest. (For this reason, some people refer to folk magic as practical magic.) Passed along as oral tradition, its practices vary from place to place, and witches generally do not feel constrained to follow them to the letter. In addition, folk magic does not usually require special

Unlike witches in stories who create magic mixtures of such odd and creepy ingredients as spider eggs and eye of newt, practitioners of folk magic gather easy-to-find items to make charms and potions. Stones, feathers, and herbs are common elements used in practical magic.

ritualistic tools. Instead, its practitioners use everyday objects—such as feathers, eggshells, or herbs.

This relaxed easiness makes folk magic popular with contemporary witches. As Sarah Anne Lawless, a witch who practices folk magic, writes,

> The beauty of folk magic is that it is practical magic. Don't have an obscure magical herb for a spell? No worries, find something already in your pantry or yard instead. Don't have a special anointing oil for your candle spell? No worries, use olive oil. Lacking a specific incense for a ritual? You guessed it . . . there's something in your kitchen cupboard to burn in its place.[6]

The common items associated with earlier folk magic, however, might seem strange to contemporary practitioners. An example of such an item is the witch bottle, once used to trap harmful intentions and spirits of the dead or the living. Historians believe that these bottles were first used during the seventeenth century. In 1681 English clergyman Joseph Glanvill wrote about one such device while relating advice given by an old man skilled in folk magic to a husband whose wife was being haunted by a spirit that was making her sick. Glanvill reports, "The Old Man bid him and his Wife be of good courage. It was but a dead Spright, he said, and he would put him in a course to rid his Wife of this languishment and trouble. He therefore advised him to take a Bottle, and put his Wives Urine into it, together with Pins and Needles and Nails, and Cork them up and set the Bottle to the Fire well corkt."[7]

The bottle contained the victim's urine as a way to trick a ghostly spirit or a witch's spirit into believing the victim was in the bottle. Other things associated with the victim, such as snippets of hair or nail clippings, might be used instead. The spirit

> "The beauty of folk magic is that it is practical magic. Don't have an obscure magical herb for a spell? No worries, find something already in your pantry or yard instead. Don't have a special anointing oil for your candle spell? No worries, use olive oil."[6]
>
> —*Witch Sarah Anne Lawless.*

A witch bottle from the 1800s is displayed along with some of its contents. The bottle—filled with personal items such as hair clippings—served as a lure to trick evil spirits into entering the container instead of the person who supplied the clippings.

would then go into the bottle, become stuck on the pins, and be destroyed in the fire with the bottle. However, after this magic cure was complete, the woman was still sick. Consequently, the old man advised the husband to try preparing another bottle and burying it in the earth. This time the spirit was trapped forever and the woman became well, but the end of her curse brought the death of a man in a nearby town. Glanvill explains that this man "was a Wizzard, and had bewitched this Mans Wife and that this Counter-practice prescribed by the Old Man, which saved the Mans Wife from languishment, was the death of that Wizzard that had bewitched her."[8]

Magical Objects

Other types of magical objects from years past are still common today. This is the case with charms, amulets, and talismans. These are objects that have been imbued with magic power. When they are worn or carried, they impart the benefits of their magic to the person who has them. The object is often a piece of jewelry, but it could be something else instead. Charms are made for a single purpose, such as to attract love, to bring wealth, to increase creativity, or to strengthen psychic gifts. An amulet is usually intended to protect its wearer from harm, danger, or illness. A talisman is usually intended to bring good luck or some other benefit.

The oldest-known use of magic associated with the Christian faith is a charm in the form of a piece of papyrus that is over fifteen hundred years old. Meant to be folded and tucked into a locket, the papyrus contains biblical writings, in Greek, intended to confer protection on the person wearing the locket. Experts believe that the charm was made in sixth-century Egypt, in a village then known as Hermopolis (now Al Ashmunin).

Spells

People who practice magic have long believed that words have power. This is why most magic spells involve spoken words or phrases. Also called incantations, spells can be performed, or cast, by chanting, speaking, or mentally reciting these words or phrases in a certain order while focusing mental energy on a desired result. This result can be for the person casting the spell or for someone else.

Modern witches generally believe that the words in their spells are calling on either supernatural forces in the universe or deities to bring about changes in circumstances. During the Middle Ages and Renaissance, however, sorcerers (men who practiced high magic) used spells to call on specific demons or angels whom they then expected to do their bidding.

Some spells are fairly standard. These are passed from one person to another or appear in grimoires, which are books of

The Cat in the Wall

In 2011, near Pendle Hill in Lancashire, England, utility workers discovered a seventeenth-century cottage under a grass mound. They called in archaeologists, who found the remains of a cat that had been bricked into the wall of a sealed room. The archaeologists said that the cat would likely have been walled in alive as a way to protect the residents from evil spirits.

Evidence suggests that the house was inhabited as late as the nineteenth century, but no one knows who put the cat in the wall. Archaeologists suspect that the cottage was once the home of either the Device or the Chattox family. The two families, both of which made their living as healers, had a long-standing rivalry and were associated with a series of witch trials that took place in 1612. Specifically, a member of the Device family named Alizon was accused of bewitching a peddler for refusing to sell her some pins. She tried to save herself by telling the local magistrate that the Chattox family had done far worse: they had killed four people by witchcraft. Members of the Chattox family then accused Alizon's grandmother of killing people by witchcraft. During his investigation, the local magistrate discovered that the Device family had held a party on Good Friday, when Christians were supposed to be at church. The partygoers were accused of witchcraft and were arrested. Many of the accused from both families eventually confessed to the crime of witchcraft, and ten were hanged as witches.

magic spells. Other spells are created by individual witches for specific occasions. In either case, the words of the spell have been chosen very carefully because practitioners of magic believe that a spell must be specific, detailed, and clear in order to avoid bringing about unintended results. For example, a spell that simply asks for a lot of money might bring about the death of a beloved relative who has included the spell caster in his or her will. To avoid these types of unpleasant outcomes, contemporary witches typically add some kind of phrase to a spell that asks that the intended result come about with joy and peace.

Many contemporary witches also believe that spells will be stronger and more effective if certain actions are performed during their casting. Likewise, they believe that some spells will not work at all if these actions are not performed. Actions might include lighting a candle, tying a knot, or walking in a certain direction. If objects like candles are used, sometimes a witch will ritually charge them with magic first.

Healing Magic

Just as each spell has a specific purpose, so too do different types of magic. Consequently, types of magic have been labeled in terms of what they are intended to do as opposed to how they are performed. For example, magic intended to help people is called white magic, and magic intended to harm people is called black magic. Similarly, magic intended to seek knowledge of the future is known as divination; magic intended to bring about communications with the dead is called necromancy, and magic intended to heal the body or the spirit is simply known as healing magic.

Healing magic has been practiced at least since ancient times, whether by priests or sorcerers skilled in high magic or by wise folk with knowledge of herbs. Methods of healing have varied over the centuries, but many have included the use of herbs and the uttering of a spell. In folk magic, sometimes the person with the illness is required to perform a certain action in order to get well. For example, one cure requires the sufferer to boil an egg and bury it in an anthill; it is believed that once the ants have consumed the egg, the person's illness will be gone.

Divination

Divination has long been used in cultures and countries worldwide. Its popularity is understandable since, in an unpredictable world, it can be comforting for people to think they know what the future holds for them. However, witches disagree on the best way to divine the future, and some forms of divination have fallen out of favor over the centuries.

One form that was once common but is now relatively obscure is geomancy. This involves a ritual whereby a handful of dirt, rocks, or sand is thrown on the ground so that lines, textures, and other features in the substance can be "read" to foretell the future. During the Renaissance, geomancy was considered one of seven types of magic known collectively as the forbidden arts. The others—many of them also relatively rare today—are hydromancy (divination via throwing stones in a pool and reading the ripples and other features of the water), aeromancy (reading cloud formations and other aspects of the air), pyromancy (reading flames or sacrificial fires, sometimes after throwing salt or herbs into the fire), chiromancy (also known as palm reading), and spatulamancy or scapulimancy (reading the shoulder bones of animals, sometimes after the animal has been ritually sacrificed and the bones have been burned).

Three of the most common methods of divination among contemporary witches are runes, tarot cards, and scrying. The latter requires the practitioner to stare into a reflective object or a container of liquid, both of which are called a speculum, until a vision appears. Speculums include black bowls of water; glass or crystal balls in colors such as dark blue, dark green, or deep lavender; mirrors whose backs have been painted black; and polished stones or gems. According to practitioners, these visions usually appear within the reflective surface, but they might also appear within the practitioner's mind. In either case, they might be images related to future events, or they might provide information to solve current problems, such as finding a lost object or making a difficult decision.

Contemporary witches generally believe that certain practices must be followed for scrying to work. In particular, most witches think that a speculum will do nothing unless it is first consecrated in a ritual performed under a full moon. Many further believe that the speculum must never be exposed to bright light, particularly direct sunlight, or it will lose its power. Therefore, they say, it must be stored in a box or kept wrapped in dark cloth.

Runes and Tarot Cards

Some witches store runes and tarot cards in a box or bag made of a natural substance for the same reason—that is, to ensure

Secret Occult Orders

Occultism is the belief in and study of the occult—the supernatural, the mystical, and the magical. People who study the occult often belong to secret societies, many of which are devoted to ceremonial magic. Perhaps the most famous of these is the Hermetic Order of the Golden Dawn, a ceremonial magic order founded in London, England, in 1888. (*Hermetic* means "relating to an ancient occult tradition.") Two of its founders, occultist Samuel Liddel Mathers and coroner William Wynn Westcott, had also been initiated into two other secret societies, the Freemasons and the Rosicrucians. The third founder was retired physician William Robert Woodman.

In establishing Golden Dawn's system of teaching magic, the order drew upon Rosicrucian beliefs, which hark back to ancient Egyptian myths, magic, and traditions. However, in addition to its ancient Egyptian teachings, Golden Dawn educates its members on other magical and mystical systems. These include Enochian magic, a system of ceremonial magic based on the evocation and commanding of spirits; theurgy, which includes magic rituals to invoke gods and the divine; and Hermetic Qabalah, an occult and mystical tradition arising out of Jewish kabbalah (which arose out of Jewish mysticism); pagan religions; and other influences.

that their magic powers will remain strong. Most also perform cleansing rituals over these items prior to their use, perhaps followed by an empowerment ritual that will charge the objects with their owner's energy. Cleansing and empowerment might involve sprinkling the object with salt or passing it through the smoke of a fire in order to connect it to the power of the elements of earth and fire.

Runes are characters of the earliest written alphabet of Germanic peoples in Europe and Scandinavia. In ancient times only pagan priests knew the meaning of these characters, each of which was connected to joy, prosperity, protection, or some other state of being. Both then and now, runes are employed in making charms and magic spells; their magic is evoked when they are marked on certain objects.

For purposes of divination, runes are typically marked on small stones, crystals, or sticks, and each rune is considered to have a complex meaning in terms of past, present, and future events. A person randomly selects a certain number of runes while concentrating on a question related to whatever he or she wants to learn from them. For example, the question might be, "What will happen if I change jobs?" The order in which the runes are selected, and the meaning of each rune, will help determine the answer to the question. However, one rune, called *wyrd*, is blank; its name means that the answer to the question is unknowable.

Tarot cards are a deck of seventy-eight cards portraying various images and symbols that are believed to be connected to ancient magic. One theory holds that around 1200 CE, occultists from throughout the civilized world gathered in Morocco to develop a way to pass on their teachings, and the earliest tarot cards were their solution. Specifically, they placed their most magical images and symbols on the cards, many of which came from a magical system, the kabbalah, thought to have been developed by the ancient Hebrews.

There are two types of tarot cards within the deck, the major arcana and the minor arcana. Each of the four suits of fourteen cards in the minor arcana represents one of the four elements used in magic (earth, air, fire, and water) as well as a set of traits related to that element. For example, the cards that symbolize fire (the suit of wands) represent power and energy, and those that symbolize water (the suit of cups) represent emotions and good luck. Each of the twenty-two cards in the major arcana bears an image representing a person, object, or situation, such as the cards of the high priestess, the wheel of fortune, and strength, respectively.

Cards are drawn and laid on a table in a prescribed pattern, and a card's position influences its meaning. For example, if the death card appears in a layout position representing the past, it would mean that the person for whom the reading is being performed has already gone through some sort of change or disaster. If the card appears in a position representing the future, it means that this event is yet to occur. The meaning of each card is also open to interpretation based on the circumstances of the person for whom the cards are being read. For example, the death card might mean a physical death, a personal disaster, an ending of something, or a transition from one phase of life to the next.

Some witches use tarot cards to read a person's future or answer specific questions the individual might have. The seventy-eight cards have distinctive suits and symbols that have different meanings depending on how they are drawn and arranged.

The Sources of Magic

In the hands of an experienced user, tarot cards can sometimes provide strikingly accurate predictions of an individual's future. But people disagree on where these messages come from—and, indeed, on where all magic comes from. Is magic the result of some real power, or is it simply coincidence or chance? Some witches think it comes from a mysterious force in the universe, others from a deity, and still others from a force within the human mind.

In any case, many witches believe that magic cannot work without energy. As witch Lynn Windsor states, "Magic is the process by which change occurs. Energy is the substance that causes that change. So, theoretically, if you could remove the process by which energy is used, you could eliminate magic."[9]

Many witches also believe that because the elements of earth, air, fire, and water are the essence of all life, they create magical energy when their forces are combined. In fact, Anne Mia Steno of the Danish Folklore Archives, who has studied present-day witches in Scandinavia, says, "The witches believe that everything in our surroundings contains energy: the ground, air, stones, etc. By using magic it is possible to 'bend', i.e. influence, the energy with a view to using it for a specific purpose."[10]

Steno adds that this means rituals exist only to serve the magic, not vice versa. As she explains, "Most witches believe they can bend the energy by the power of thought alone. This means that it's not necessary to summon a god or perform a ritual for the magic to work. So when they perform rituals during a full moon, the idea is to focus their thoughts to make the magic stronger. The magic isn't really in the ritual itself."[11]

A Successful Outcome?

When such focus is followed by the desired outcome, witches are certain that their magic has worked. When the outcome does not occur, witches typically fault the way the spell was performed. Perhaps the witch did not focus enough on the intent or had some doubt over whether the spell would work, thereby weakening the magic, or maybe the area where the spell was cast was not properly prepared.

Some witches insist that they have also had evidence during spell casting that there is magic present. This evidence might be in the form of small signs, such as a candle inexplicably blowing out or an object moving with no apparent cause. But there are also reports of large signs. For example, ghost expert Paul Dale Roberts tells of unexplained phenomena experienced by some witches while chanting to Thor, the Norse god of sky and thunder. Roberts says,

> The more they chanted, the night became stormy. The presence of Thor was felt and all of a sudden, it started to rain in buckets, the heavy winds blew wildly and the tarp that gave them shelter blew to the ground. When the chanting [subsided], everything went back to normal. They later learned that there was no other storm anywhere else, the storm only hit the location of where the Circle was at.[12]

However, Roberts did not witness this event for himself, and skeptics say that any such report not witnessed by someone outside the coven is suspect. It could be a fabrication, they point out, or an exaggeration or delusion. And in the case of a storm occurring while a god of storms is being invoked, it could merely be the result of coincidence and the fact that the invocation was taking place while the storm was already brewing. Skeptics can come up with many alternate explanations for the things that witches say have occurred because of their magic.

"When [witches] perform rituals during a full moon, the idea is to focus their thoughts to make the magic stronger. The magic isn't really in the ritual itself."[11]

—Anne Mia Steno of the Danish Folklore Archives.

People who think that witches and witchcraft are evil can come up with other explanations as well. They say that magic is not a natural force but an unnatural one. Specifically, they say that it comes from the devil. Moreover, some say that it does not genuinely work but that the devil merely tricks people into thinking that it works. Others say that it does work but that the devil makes witches think they are performing beneficial magic when actually their magic ends up harming unsuspecting victims and possibly the witch as well.

Contemporary witches reject such notions, however, because they do not believe that the devil exists. They also ignore the skeptics because they say that they have seen magic at work. They know it is real, they insist, and that their witchcraft brings genuine results.

Chapter 2

Why Do People Believe in Witchcraft?

"Witches ar servantes onelie [only], and slaues [slaves] to the Devil."

—King James VI of Scotland.

Quoted in Lara Apps and Andrew Gow, *Male Witches in Early Modern Europe*. Manchester, UK: Manchester University Press, 2003, p. 149.

"My mother is a witch and that I know to be true. I have seen her spirit in the likeness of a brown dog, which she called Ball."

—Jennet Device, nine, testifying during a 1612 witch trial in England.

Quoted in Frances Cronin, "The Witch Trial That Made Legal History," BBC News, August 17, 2011. www.bbc.com.

In contemporary society, people who identify themselves as witches are sometimes looked down upon for believing that their witchcraft produces real magic. But at one time, believing in witchcraft was the norm. In fact, over time there have probably been more believers in magic than nonbelievers. Moreover, some experts say that even people who identify themselves as skeptics believe in magic, whether secretly or subconsciously.

Magical Thinking

One such expert is psychology writer Matthew Hutson, author of *The 7 Laws of Magical Thinking*. After studying years of research related to belief systems, Hutson concludes that it is natural for humans to think that they are the cause of certain events that are actually caused by chance. He reports, "We tend to assume that if something happened, it was caused by an agent. If we don't see any biological agent, like a person or animal, then we might assume that there's some sort of invisible agent: God or the universe in general with a mind of its own."[13]

Hutson says that humans likely developed this tendency to look for the cause of something because it helps keep them safe. That is, it compels people to pay more attention to their surroundings while looking for what might have caused the action, and this prevents them from being unsuspecting prey.

Hutson also reports that humans share a tendency to think that symbolic actions create real actions. This is the thinking behind using a voodoo doll to hurt someone. Believers in voodoo think that pins stuck in the doll injure the person represented by the doll in the same locations on the body. Hutson says, "When you do some symbolic action or perform some symbolic ritual, you tend to think it will bring about what it symbolizes."[14] This is the basis of a belief in magic—thinking that a particular ritual will cause whatever the ritual is intended to cause.

In discussing Hutson's work, science writer Natalie Wolchover suggests that such thinking has been beneficial to the survival of the human race. She says,

> Even the most die-hard skeptics among us believe in magic. Humans can't help it: though we try to be logical, irrational beliefs—many of which we aren't even conscious of—are hardwired in our psyches. But rather than hold us back, the unavoidable habits of mind that make us think luck and supernatural forces are real, that objects and

> "We tend to assume that if something happened, it was caused by an agent. If we don't see any biological agent, like a person or animal, then we might assume that there's some sort of invisible agent: God or the universe in general with a mind of its own."[13]
>
> —*Psychology writer Matthew Hutson, author of* The 7 Laws of Magical Thinking.

symbols have power, and that humans have souls and destinies are part of what has made our species so evolutionarily successful. Believing in magic is good for us.[15]

Ancient Egypt

Perhaps for this reason, a belief in magic has existed since the first recorded history. Among the earliest evidence of this are ancient Egyptian funerary writings. For example, the Coffin Texts are magic spells that were written on coffins, tomb walls, and other funerary objects. There are over one thousand of these spells, and some of them come in long and short versions.

Another collection of spells is the Papyri Graecae Magicae, written on Egyptian papyri dating from between the second century BCE and fifth century CE. As with modern spells, these ancient Egyptian spells had a variety of purposes, such as healing, bringing love, and imparting immortality. Also like modern spells, ancient Egyptian spells usually involved speaking certain words, often while performing certain actions such as using a wand to draw a protective circle around someone or pouring water over a wound.

Different types of spells were performed by different types of practitioners. For example, the lector (reader) priests—so named because they were among the few literate Egyptians and could therefore read the books of magic kept in temples and palaces— cast spells to protect the king and help the deceased be reborn. Priests who served the goddess of plague, Sekhmet, specialized in healing magic. Scorpion charmers used magic to drive away poisonous reptiles and scorpions, and wise women used magic to deal with troublesome ghosts.

Curses

To the ancient Egyptians, spells were meant to benefit individuals and society. Nonetheless, sometimes a spell was cast for evil purposes. For example, when Ramses III was ruler of Egypt (from

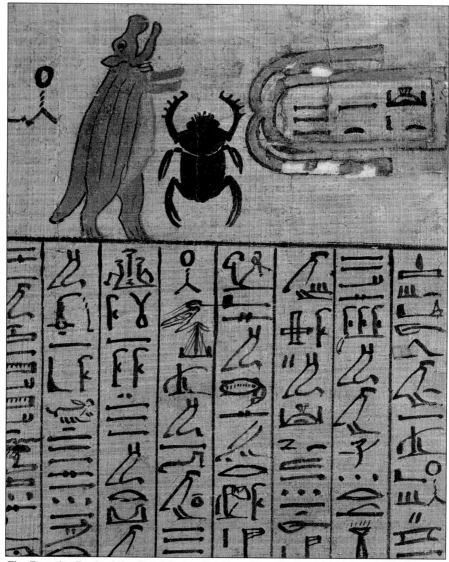

The Egyptian Book of the Dead *is a collection of spells compiled by ancient priests over a thousand years. Surviving images of these spells on tomb walls, sarcophagi, and fragments of papyrus show hieroglyph-filled incantations that were used to help the dead pass through the underworld into the afterlife.*

about 1187 to 1156 BCE), some priests attempted to kill the king and his bodyguards using magic spells, potions, and figurines. There were also cases of Egyptians casting evil spells for financial gain, particularly after the country became a Roman province in 30 BCE.

The practice of casting evil spells in exchange for money also occurred in ancient Greece, prompting the Greek scholar Plato (who lived from roughly 428 to 348 BCE) to write, "If anyone wishes to injure an enemy, at a small cost he may harm just and unjust indifferently; for with their incantations and magic formulae they say they can persuade the Gods to serve their will."[16] In fact, although Greeks also used spells for beneficial purposes—particularly healing and attracting love—a great deal of their magic was intended to cause harm. For example, it was common to cause harm to effigies—representations, such as dolls, of specific people—in order to harm the individuals they were intended to represent. Curse tablets were also common. By writing spells on a tablet, it was believed that people's actions could be restricted in some way (such as making them unable to give testimony in a legal case). Curses were also used to make people suffer great pain. To protect themselves from such spells, people often carried amulets and charms designed to shield them from evil magic.

Charlatans?

The Roman philosopher Pliny the Elder (23–79 CE) called those who performed evil magic for a fee charlatans. However, he did not doubt that magic was real, or that certain people were genuinely skilled in sorcery, only that some individuals faked such skills in order to make a profit. Today, however, the common view is that all people who claim to be skilled in magic are charlatans. Much of the reason for this change in belief is due to the efforts of the Catholic Church.

As the dominant representative of the Christian faith in Europe from the fifth century to at least the fifteenth century, the Catholic Church declared that only God—and no one else—had any magical powers. In the eyes of the church, therefore, anyone who practiced sorcery or witchcraft was going against church teachings. Consequently, beginning in the ninth century the Catholic Church established penalties, such as fasting, prayers, and fines, to punish people who engaged in such practices. The church also specifically prohibited the making of potions and charms, the casting of spells, and the use of any sort of magic to prevent or end pregnancies, reduce fertility or male ardor, or attract or repel love.

Despite these efforts, church officials failed to convince people to abandon either their practice of or belief in magic. During the thirteenth century church officials established an Inquisition, a body within the judicial system of the Catholic Church, to arrest, try, and usually execute such heretics—people who went against the teachings of the Catholic Church. This was one in a series of Inquisitions that operated in various parts of the Christian world.

At first people were subjected to examinations by the church inquisitors only if there were already clear evidence that they had committed heresy. In other words, before inquisitors could interrogate someone, they needed to have solid proof that the person had genuinely been doing the things he or she was accused of doing. The Catholic Church took this approach because, according to its teachings, Satan and his demons could trick people into believing things that were not true. For example, a demon might make a self-professed witch think she was flying on a broomstick through the night to the site of a demonic ritual when, in fact, she was asleep in her bed. Therefore, the church did not assume that someone who claimed to be consorting with the devil really was.

Brutal Interrogations

In 1326, however, the Catholic Church decided to allow inquisitors to investigate cases where witchcraft and demonology were merely suspected. This meant that a person who had not been charged with heresy could be subjected to the often brutal interrogation techniques of the inquisitors. In addition, the leader of the Catholic Church, Pope John XXII, had become convinced that someone was trying to kill him via magic. He put forth a list specifying which acts of magic the inquisitors could consider to be heresy. These included making a pact with the devil and trying to summon demons. The pope believed that many people were engaging in such activities. He stated, "Grievingly we observe . . . that many who are

Superstition as an Excuse

In India between the years 2000 and 2012, over two thousand people died at the hands of angry mobs, vengeful relatives, or others who had accused them of practicing black magic. Some of the victims were beaten to death, some were hacked to death, and others were hanged. In many cases, they were also brutally tortured prior to their deaths. Experts say that the vast majority of these deaths are not really about fear and superstition. According to Pooja Singhal Purwar, a social welfare official, "Superstition is only an excuse. Often a woman is branded a witch so that you can throw her out of the village and grab her land, or to settle scores, family rivalry, or because powerful men want to punish her for spurning their sexual advances. Sometimes, it is used to punish women who question social norms."

Quoted in Terrence McCoy, "Thousands of Women, Accused of Sorcery, Tortured and Executed in Indian Witch Hunts," *Washington Post,* July 21, 2014. www.washington post.com.

Christians in name only . . . sacrifice to demons, adore them, make or have made images, rings, mirrors . . . for magic purposes, and bind themselves to demons. They ask and receive responses from them and to fulfill their most depraved lusts ask them for aid . . . and make a pact with hell."[17]

Many members of the Catholic Church believed this as well, but the pope's comments caused still more people to associate witchcraft with Satanism. This association is understandable given not only Christians' firm belief in Satan but also the harsh circumstances of medieval life. People suffered many seemingly unexplainable misfortunes—crops failed, children died in infancy, illnesses ran rampant. At the same time, they felt that if they lived in accordance with God's will then he would protect and reward them. When this did not happen, they blamed the personification of evil, Satan, and the witches who supposedly served him through their magical arts.

As Christianity came to dominate Europe, the church deemed witchcraft a practice that conflicted with the power of God. Therefore, the clergy quickly aligned magic with satanic corruption. Witches and anyone suspected of sorcery were routinely hunted down as disciples of the devil.

Weak Women

The idea that witches were associates of Satan soon supplanted the image of witches as healers. And because Satan was believed to be both a trickster and more powerful than humans, people also began to think that Satan was responsible for any magic that might be produced through witchcraft. In other words, Satan was merely using witches as conduits for evil magic. As an example of how Satan might use witches, when the Black

Death (bubonic plague) swept through Europe beginning in 1346, a popular theory was that members of a secret organization of witches were being directed by the devil to poison water wells, thereby sickening people throughout Europe.

The Catholic Church's position was that the plague was not caused by human beings but by God as a punishment for people's sins. But because the plague struck down innocents as well as sinners, many of Europe's inhabitants doubted that God could be the cause. Consequently, they wrote theological arguments attempting to prove that witches could indeed cause illnesses and other evils.

One of the most significant works of this period is the *Formicarius*, thought to be only the second book to discuss witchcraft ever printed. Written by German theologian Johannes Nider between 1435 and 1437, it supported the common view that because most witches were women and therefore uneducated (as was the norm during medieval times), they lacked the ability to perform complicated magic rituals. However, Nider argued that it was not necessary to perform such rituals in order to produce magic. All that was necessary was an association with Satan. Nider also said that as the weaker sex, women were easier than men for the devil to influence, making it more likely that women would perform evil magic.

The idea that women could be capable of such evil was upsetting to many medieval people, as was the idea that Satan was the means by which a woman's magical abilities came into being. And as other scholars built on this notion, people became increasingly concerned about how to tell whether a woman was in league with the devil. Some looked to German Catholic clergymen Heinrich Kramer and Jacob Sprenger's book *Malleus Maleficarum* (*The Hammer of the Witches*), published in 1487, for help in this matter. It provided guidelines for finding witches, interrogating them, and prosecuting them. It also advocated the torture of witnesses to witchcraft and accused witches, even children. This was because Kramer believed that the battle against Satan was important enough to warrant any tactics necessary to gain confessions of evil acts.

Strengthening Belief

By the time *Malleus Maleficarum* was published, widespread attempts to find and convict witches were already well under way in Western Europe, but Kramer's work convinced witch-hunters there to deal with suspected witches more severely. This resulted in more arrests, confessions, and prosecutions, all of which strengthened people's belief in witchcraft. It also resulted in harsher penalties for witchcraft. For example, in England in 1542 Parliament passed a law defining the practice as a crime punishable by death.

No one knows exactly how many people were executed as a result of such laws. However, the most common contemporary estimate is roughly one hundred thousand deaths in Europe from 1500 through 1650, with the majority of witch trials taking place between 1580 and 1630. Since many of these trials featured convincing testimony that resulted in a conviction, they left little doubt in the minds of the general population that witches could exert great power over their friends and neighbors.

Many rulers shared this belief in the power of witches. Among the most influential was the ruler of Scotland and England, called King James VI in Scotland and James I in England. His opinion that witches were powerful and dangerous was largely forged by events that occurred between 1589 and 1590 involving his then fiancée (later queen consort), Anne of Denmark. While attempting to sail to Scotland for her marriage, she experienced several powerful storms that delayed her voyage. Later King James was sailing the North Sea when a terrible storm struck his ship as well. Shortly thereafter he presided over a witch trial in which a woman confessed that, together with other witches and at the command of Satan, she had conjured up the storm in order to kill the king.

Doubting the truth of this confession, King James demanded that the woman somehow prove that she had supernatural powers. At the time, he was not absolutely certain that witchcraft was real. Consequently, when the woman on trial told the king something in private that only he and his wife could know, the king was stunned—and he took the witch's words as proof that witchcraft was something to be feared.

Protecting King James

In 2014 restorers of Knole House, a six-hundred-year-old estate in Kent, England, found some unusual marks hidden under floorboards of rooms intended to be used by King James I during visits to Thomas Sackville, his treasurer. Sackville had received Knole House from his cousin, Queen Elizabeth I; James I was her successor. Since the king feared an attack by witchcraft, when the new rooms were added they included witch marks for his protection. According to the UK newspaper the *Guardian,*

> Archaeologists found the marks not just in the bed chamber prepared for James, but carved into the joists and around the fireplace of the room directly overhead, which would probably have been occupied by one of his sons or a close member of his retinue. . . . The marks, made in the enormous oak beams on the sides facing the fireplace—for the superstitious, a known weak spot in defence against witches—include scorch marks made with a candle flame before the timbers were installed, carved tangles of Vs and Ws invoking the protection of the Virgin Mary, and maze-like marks known as demon traps, intended to trap the malevolent spirits which would follow the lines and be unable to find their way back out.

However, Sackville died shortly after the new rooms were completed, and James's anticipated visit never occurred.

Maev Kennedy, "Witch Marks Fit for a King Beguile Archaeologists at Knole," *Guardian,* November 4, 2014. www.theguardian.com.

King James then became obsessed with making sure that everyone else shared his view of witches. He particularly wanted to counter works like English author Reginald Scott's 1584 book, *The Discoverie of Witchcraft,* which argued that most of the people prosecuted as witches had no supernatural powers. Instead,

Scott argued, most were either innocent victims or people deluded into thinking they had powers. The rest, he suggested, had merely pretended to have magic powers for reasons of financial gain, or they had claimed to kill someone using a magic spell when, in fact, they had used poison.

Expressing Disbelief

Scott also said that anyone who expressed a belief that witches had magic powers was going against God, whether or not that person actually used the services of a witch. Specifically, he wrote, "He that attributeth to a witch, such divine power, as duly and only appertaineth unto GOD . . . is in heart a blasphemer, an idolater, and full of gross impiety, although he neither go nor send to her for assistance."[18] This statement angered King James, who tried unsuccessfully to destroy every copy of the book in existence.

The king was also upset that many of his subjects had been convinced by Scott's arguments. He therefore wrote his own book to rebut Scott's. Published in 1597 as *Daemonologie*, the king's work described the powers of witches—including the ability to cause storms—and provided guidelines for the examination, testing, prosecution, and execution of witches.

In addition, scholars commissioned by the king to produce a new translation of the Bible chose words that would make it seem as though the condemnation of witches was ordained by God. For example, in the King James Version of the Bible, the Old Testament Book of Exodus states, "Thou shalt not suffer a witch to live" (Exod. 22:28). However, "witch" should have been translated from the original Hebrew version and the Latin translations that followed as either "poisoner" or "evil sorcerer." After the King James Version was published in 1611, the biblical command to "not suffer a witch to live" became one of the most common justifications for executing witches, not only in Scotland and England but in other parts of the world as well.

Nonetheless, there were also those who questioned the motives behind witch accusations. For example, an inquisitor in Spain, Alonso de Salazar Frías, earned the nickname "the Witches' Advocate" because he argued that accusations against purported witches were typically based on dreams and fantasies. In fact, after examining nearly two thousand cases of witchcraft accusations, he declared, "I have not found a single proof nor even the slightest indication from which to infer that one act of witchcraft has actually taken place."[19] In 1611 Salazar also noted that accusations increased dramatically in the aftermath of sermons about the dangers of witchcraft, suggesting that such preaching whipped up witch hysteria among the general public. As a result of Salazar's report on this matter, the Catholic Church in Spain prohibited priests from giving sermons on witchcraft.

A Persistent Belief

Witch hysteria declined in the Western world during the late seventeenth and early eighteenth centuries. As a result, various countries changed their laws and practices regarding witch persecution. For example, France abolished the crime of witchcraft in 1682, and the last witch executions occurred in England and Scotland, respectively, in 1684 and 1722. Therefore, historian James Hannam reports, "by the late 17th century witch trials were already reasonably rare occurrences even in the same localities where, in the earlier part of that century, the greatest hunts had taken place."[20]

> "Belief is a notoriously hard thing to measure, but almost all societies appear to have some tradition of witches and fear of magic has been nearly universal."[21]
>
> —Historian James Hannam.

However, Hannam adds, "The decline in trials and hunts did not necessarily presage a corresponding decline in the belief in witches just as their start did not correspond to any increase. Belief is a notoriously hard thing to measure, but almost all societies appear to have some tradition of witches and fear of magic has been nearly universal."[21] In other words, even as witch hunts ended, the belief that witches had supernatural powers persisted.

This belief persists today. As Natalie Wolchover notes, studies by Matthew Hutson and others indicate that there will always be a certain percentage of the population that believes in witchcraft: "Most of us try our best to be rational. But, the research suggests, remnants of the magical thinking we evolved with invariably creep in."[22]

Fear and Ignorance

Moreover, the same kind of fear and ignorance that led to witch trials in centuries past continues to exist in modern times. As an example of this, in Papua New Guinea illnesses and deaths that rural villagers cannot explain are often blamed on witchcraft. The trials of accused witches are extremely brief, unjust affairs that typically end in gruesome executions carried out by a mob.

Cultural and religious influences can also contribute to a belief in witchcraft in the modern world. In Saudi Arabia, for example, witch executions are based on the teachings of the Koran, the sacred book of Islam. Those teachings condemn witchcraft. As Abdullah Jaber, a political cartoonist at the Saudi daily newspaper *Al-Jazirah*, explains, "In accordance with our Islamic tradition we believe that magic really exists. . . . [Even our] government recognizes this, like Muslims worldwide." Yet Jaber adds that although most older people, especially those in rural areas, believe in magic, many well-educated Saudis do not, despite the teachings of their religion. He states, "It's a matter of ignorance. If people were more educated they wouldn't believe in this."[23]

> "Most of us try our best to be rational. But, the research suggests, remnants of the magical thinking we evolved with invariably creep in."[22]
>
> — Science writer Natalie Wolchover.

However, an international study conducted in South Africa and reported in 2012 suggests that even educated people can blame witchcraft for their misfortunes. Led by psychologist Cristine H. Legare of the University of Texas, Austin, this study involved interviewing South Africans about their views related to the AIDS virus. Although most of those interviewed knew the medical explanation for how the disease is transmitted because it is a se-

In Papua New Guinea many rural islanders still believe that some misfortunes are caused by witchcraft. In 2013 a female teacher was accused of being a witch and publically beheaded by a mob that believed her evil spells had brought about the death of a sick villager.

rious health problem in the country, they thought that witchcraft was involved as well. In fact, many said that they probably got the disease because a witch made sure they interacted with a carrier.

Gaining Advantages

Studies have also suggested that the more unhappy people are with their lives, the more likely they are to believe in witchcraft. Some experts say this is because unhappy people tend to view themselves as victims of bad luck, and people would rather attribute their misfortune to a witch's curse than to randomness. Others say that unhappy people believe in magic because they see it as a way to end their unhappiness, perhaps by using a spell to gain wealth or love. Indeed, studies have shown that when times are hard, the number of people who dabble in witchcraft goes up.

Anne-Maria Makhulu, an assistant professor of cultural anthropology at Duke University, adds that a belief in magic can also give people hope of changes to come. She explains, "People believe in magic for all sorts of reasons, including the desire to accrue wealth or advance in life, but the belief also says something about a deep-seated human desire for equality. When people say they believe in magical forces, they believe in magic that can make the world equal and just in circumstances where it's not."[24] In other words, a belief in magic can be an expression of hope for those who are disadvantaged in life.

Chapter 3

Is Witchcraft More Myth than Magic?

"Myths describe the various and sometimes dramatic break-throughs of the sacred (or the 'supernatural') into the World. It is this sudden breakthrough of the sacred that really establishes the World and makes it what it is today."

—Romanian historian Mircea Eliade.
Quoted in David Cave, *Mircea Eliade's Vision for a New Humanism*, Oxford, UK: Oxford University Press, 1992, p. 68.

"Myths are fun, as long as you don't confuse them with the truth."

—Evolutionary biologist Richard Dawkins.
Quoted in *Duke Today*, "Richard Dawkins Extols the 'Magic of Reality,'" March 30, 2012. http://m.today.duke.edu.

Experts disagree on just how much contemporary witchcraft is like the witchcraft of old. They also disagree on whether modern-day perceptions of early witchcraft are accurate. This is because myths featuring witches have become intermingled with historical facts, making it difficult to separate fiction from truth.

The Products of Witch Hunts

One of the reasons why myth and fact became mixed is because much of the information about witchcraft was acquired from witch hunts, with their associated false accusations and acts of torture to extract confessions. As the website Faust.com, a forum for discussions related to magic, reports, "There never really was witchcraft as we imagine it—those definitions came out of the fright and zeal of the Inquisitors and the public, and consequently, witchcraft magically disappeared the day the last of the fires went out, like a phantom."[25] (In Europe and North America, witch hunts took place from roughly the mid-fifteenth century to the mid- to late eighteenth century depending on location.)

Indeed, once the witch hysteria that triggered witch hunts disappeared, so too did the practice of witchcraft—at least on the surface. Undoubtedly, the witch hunts had taught at least some witches the value of practicing in secret. But Faust .com suggests that even before witchcraft apparently went underground, it was not a true practice. That is, it was not a single collection of beliefs and practices. The website states, "The history of witchcraft is dubious. It may be a catch-all phrase for innumerable, disparate local practices that came to be known generally as witchcraft when the harrowing of the witch hunts created a popular definition of witchcraft."[26]

The Elements of Myth

Another reason that views about premodern witches could be skewed is that some of what is known about witches comes from myths—traditional stories typically about supernatural beings and events. Although some experts think there are elements of truth in these stories, many say they are wholly made up. In either case, historians say that Christians, who believe in one god, promoted certain myths as the complete truth in order to paint witches, many of whom were pagans and therefore believed in many gods, in a bad light. Angela Sangster, an expert on the paranormal, reports that "tales began to be told of these 'creatures of Satan,' usually female, who would make pacts with the Devil to live a life of sorcery and magic . . . and in service to him. As time went on, even more mythologies were mixed in to justify a fear of witches."[27]

Sangster also reports that witch-hunters used myths to encourage more witch accusations and executions. She says, "Of all the wrongs done in the name of God . . . the mass hysteria of the 'evils of witches' that took place in the Middle Ages throughout Europe and colonial America is among the worst. In an effort to sway public opinion to support the Church in all ways . . . these myths of witches being evil and Satanic were fostered by these leaders."[28]

Indeed, in promoting the idea that witches were foul creatures, the Catholic Church had many mythological figures upon which to draw. An example of this is Baba Yaga, a powerful witch of Slavic folklore. An ugly, deformed, frightening old woman who lives in a hut in the forest, she is often described as having iron teeth, chicken legs, and a desire to eat people. Such figures helped establish

A bony crone from Slavic folklore, Baba Yaga is often portrayed as having a long nose and long, pointed teeth. Such descriptions of witch-like women in fables helped the Catholic Church characterize all witches as foul, ugly creatures.

the idea that witches were ugly. Consequently, during the centuries of witch-hunting, ugly people were often accused of witchcraft. For example, in the 1640s the Reverend John Gaule said of the targets of a witch hunt in England, "Every old woman with a wrinkled face, a furr'd brow, a hairy lip, a gobber tooth, a squint eye, a squeaking voice, or a scolding tongue is not only suspected, but pronounced for a witch."[29]

Moreover, if a suspected witch had no outward signs of ugliness, then the witch was said to have hidden ones, such as moles or other skin blemishes, beneath his or her clothes. Fifteenth-century witch-hunter Lambert Daneau stated,

There is not a single witch upon whom the devil doth not set some note or token of his power and prerogative over them. . . . It is imprinted on the most secret parts of the body; with men, under the eyelids or perhaps under the armpits . . . or elsewhere; with women, it is generally on the breasts or private parts. The stamp which makes these marks is simply the devil's talon.[30]

To find these marks, accused witches were often subjected to invasive physical examinations, some of which involved shaving their hair.

Mythological Attributes

Many of the attributes that came to be associated with witches during the Middle Ages and beyond appear in myths and legends. One such attribute has to do with a witch's nature. Witches are often depicted as being evil, dishonest, and dangerous. In the myths of some cultures they are also inhuman—either beasts or creatures that are half human and half beast. In addition, there are myths in which a person seeks out a witch in order to ask the witch to hurt someone or to teach the person evil magic.

There are also many myths and legends featuring witches who engage in divination. In fact, one such witch, the Witch of Endor, appears in the Bible. At the urging of King Saul, she summons up the spirit of the prophet Samuel so that he might tell the king what will happen in an upcoming battle. The spirit predicts that not only the king but also his three sons will die—and when his sons subsequently do die, the king kills himself.

Many myths also depict witches' ability to change themselves or others into animals. An example of this is Circe from Greek mythology. A goddess of magic, she is skilled in the use of potions and herbs and uses a wand or staff to turn her enemies and offenders into animals. In Homer's epic poem *The Odyssey*, Circe uses her wand to turn the men of the legendary Greek king Odysseus into pigs, after first slipping a magic potion into their wine.

Mythological Rituals

In addition to providing ideas about witches' looks and attributes, myths have influenced people's perceptions regarding how rituals are conducted. For example, since ancient times the myths and legends of various cultures have associated frogs and toads both

Altered Mythology

In areas where Christianity replaced pagan faiths, the mythology of the ancient culture often comes to modern readers through medieval Catholic priests. These priests created written records of myths that had previously been passed down orally, and in some cases their beliefs affected their work. For example, the Norse myths that exist today were all written down around the year 1250 by priests who viewed this material—largely poetry, songs, and chants—as folklore rather than as expressions of ancient religious beliefs. Nonetheless, without the work of such priests much mythology would have been lost.

with demons and with magic. Perhaps for this reason, during the centuries of witch-hunting, many people believed that witches used these animals in their rituals. This belief appeared to be confirmed by trials where witnesses said that a certain witch had actually used such a creature.

For example, during the trial of Ursula Kemp, a wise woman and midwife who was hanged in England as a witch in 1582, her eight-year-old son testified that his mother had used a black toad in performing magic that made a boy sick. This toad, the boy said, was one of four familiars—animals that do the witch's bidding and can be used to bewitch others—used by his mother to perform magic. The others were a black cat, a gray cat, and a white lamb. Kemp subsequently confessed privately to a judge that she had indeed used familiars, either to make people sick or to kill them. Whether she was being truthful or not is unknown. Either way, it is likely that the boy's testimony was influenced more by prevailing beliefs of the time than by anything his mother might have done.

Myths have also provided information on the powers of witches. In Greek mythology, for example, witches can control the weather, bring on storms, transform people into animals, and curse a person by giving him or her the evil eye. The belief that witches can use magic to do these things has persisted for centuries, not just in Greece but in many other places as well.

The idea that witches use magic cauldrons also appears in mythology. In fact, magic cauldrons are featured prominently in Celtic mythology. In one myth, a cauldron supplies huge amounts of food but never becomes empty. In another, a magic cauldron can bring dead warriors to life.

Using Myths to Create New Traditions

Ideas drawn from myths have also been used by contemporary occultists and witches to create modern witchcraft traditions. This means that some witches practice witchcraft in ways that folklorists, historians, and other experts say are not totally accurate. As Faust.com states, "Today's 'witchcraft' is less than a few hundred years old . . . and grew out of people's imaginings about the craft—there is no substantial or substantiated tradition or continuity."[31]

Indeed, modern witchcraft draws largely upon myths and speculation about how witches once practiced their craft. Many people who describe themselves as witches today also rely on spell books and other texts of occultists, often putting their own spin on the material or cobbling together ideas from different cultures. For example, one Wiccan website reports that witches who practice Egyptian witchcraft also incorporate the concept of the wheel of the year (an annual cycle of seasonal festivals) into their rituals, a modern concept that arose from British paganism. The website also says, "Like the witch craft of any other region, the

Modern Wiccan practices often draw upon several strands of mystical beliefs and rituals from both ancient and more-modern times. According to some practitioners, the rituals and the experiences gained from them are more important than the source of the beliefs.

Bibliothèque Bleue

Advances in printing did much to increase interest in grimoires and other books on magic among the common people. In France, for example, a new type of publishing system, the *bibliothèque bleue* ("blue library"), produced inexpensive books with a blue paper cover (*livres bleus*, or "blue books"). During the late seventeenth and eighteenth centuries these included works on the occult. Consequently, even people with little money could have access to occult knowledge that was once available only to well-to-do magicians.

Moreover, according to social historian Owen Davies, over the next 150 years, mass production of *livres bleus* resulted in thousands of grimoires being circulated throughout France, spread in large part by peddlers. Among the most popular of these grimoires was *The Marvelous Secrets of Natural and Cabalistic Magic of Lesser Albert*, commonly referred to as the *Petit Albert*. (The term *cabalistic magic* refers to a form of Jewish occultism.) The Catholic Church considered this eighteenth-century work to be a book of black magic. However, some people believe that the book's author—"Lesser Albert," or Albertus Parvus Lucius, a pseudonymous narrator who claimed to have compiled writings from a variety of sources—was actually the thirteenth-century Catholic bishop (and later saint) Albertus Magnus.

Egyptian witch craft is based upon the country's tradition, myth, legend, rituals, drama, poetry, song, dance, worship, magic and living in harmony with the earth."[32] In other words, this and other traditions have been drawn from a variety of sources, at least some of them modern.

However, contemporary witches typically say that the sources of their rituals do not matter as much as the rituals themselves. According to Wiccan high priest Aidan Kelly, for witches who are also Wiccans, practices and experiences are more important than beliefs. He states, "It's a religion of ritual rather than theology. The ritual is first; the myth is second. And taking an attitude that the myths of the Craft are 'true history' in the way a fundamentalist looks at the legends of Genesis really seems crazy."[33]

The Book of Shadows

Contemporary witchcraft has also been influenced by certain personalities within the modern witchcraft movement. One such personality was Gerald Gardner, who established Wicca and its Gardnerian witchcraft tradition around 1954. He subsequently said that his witchcraft practices were based on what he had learned a few years earlier as an initiated member of an ancient, secret witch cult. However, some people believe that he made up these practices, drawing upon such sources as Celtic mythology and the writings of occultists and occult societies.

In any case, Gardner promoted the idea that witchcraft practices should be based on ancient traditions. He also created what many people believe was the first Book of Shadows, a repository of a tradition's beliefs, rules of magic, rituals, rites, incantations, spells, potions, herbalism, divination methods, and other magical practices. Largely as a result of Gardner's efforts, today each witchcraft tradition has its own version of a Book of Shadows, and every witch who belongs to a tradition has a copy of that tradition's book.

Solomon

Although Gardner is often credited with making tradition-specific books of spells, he was not the inventor of spell books. Such books existed throughout the ancient world. In fact, the ancient Greeks and Romans believed that Persian priests invented magic around the period now dated as 6347 BCE. They also believed that the first written spells, those appearing in a book from around 480 BCE, can be attributed to a Persian magician and astrologer named Osthanes.

Other examples of spells—and spell books—can be found in stories dating to biblical times. Whether they provide proof of magic or represent yet more mythical stories is uncertain. One such story revolves around Solomon, a king of Israel according to the Old Testament of the Bible and a prophet in the Koran, the sacred text of Islam. Ancient Greeks and Romans considered him a master sorcerer as well. According to Titus Flavius Josephus, a first-century Roman scholar and former slave who wrote about Jewish history, Solomon shared his knowledge by writing roughly three thousand books. Many of these, according to Josephus, included incantations and exorcisms (spells to drive away a demon that has possessed someone's body).

However, modern scholars say that the magic books purported to be by Solomon were not actually written by him. The first book attributed to Solomon, *The Testament of Solomon*, was written in Greek sometime between the first and fifth centuries CE—long after Solomon's death—most likely by someone in Egypt or Babylonia. Moreover, there is no evidence that this work was copied from an earlier text. Similarly, *The Key of Solomon,* which provides both text and drawings related to magic, surfaced in medieval times. People have long believed that it was written by Solomon, but modern historians say it dates from fourteenth- or fifteenth-century Italy.

Another popular medieval book of magic spells whose origin story seems mythic is *The Sworn Book of Honorius*, which includes spells related to contacting demons and spirits. It was said to have been written by Honorius, an ancient Greek magician from Thebes, sometime after 811 CE. At that time, according to the story of how the book came to be, magicians from Italy, Greece, and Spain held a conference at which they discussed putting all of their knowledge of magic into one text. To this end, they charged Honorius with compiling the material and making three copies of the book. Whether these books ever really existed is uncertain; copies of the originals supposedly did not appear until the thirteenth century. Furthermore, there is no evidence that Honorius ever existed.

Grimoires

Even if there is no way to confirm the existence of those earliest spell books, such books did exist centuries ago. This suggests

According to convention, King Solomon ruled in ancient Israel during the tenth century BCE. Christian and Hebrew scholars refer to Solomon as a king and the builder of the First Temple in Jerusalem. To the ancient Greeks and Romans, though, he was a sorcerer who collected many spells.

that witches, or people who identified themselves as witches, were casting spells and performing magic. Books that include spells that call upon a demon or spirit are commonly known as grimoires. The name *grimoire* comes from the Old French word *grammaire*, or "grammar," which was originally used to refer to any book written in Latin. By the eighteenth century the word was being used in France to refer to books of magic spells; by the nineteenth century the term *grimoire* was in widespread use throughout Europe. Similar works existed in other parts of the world as well, although they were called by other names.

Today people often consider a grimoire to be any book on how to perform the magic of witchcraft. However, according to Owen Davies, a professor of social history at the University of Hertfordshire and author of the book *Grimoires: A History of Magic Books,* "Not all books of magic are grimoires." He says that a grimoire needs to feature "the conjuration of spirits, the power of words, or the ritual creation of magical objects."[34] Davies also reports that grimoires that focus on the creation of magical objects, such as amulets and charms, often confine themselves to magic related to love, healing, and protection. Other grimoires concentrate on rituals and incantations used for controlling other people by summoning demons and spirits.

> "[Witches] used magick because magick worked, Gram taught Mom, who taught daughter, who taught granddaughter."[36]
>
> —Wiccans Misti Anslin Delaney and Wayland Raven.

Oral Tradition

Because contemporary witches do not believe in causing harm, attempts to control other people are not part of modern witchcraft. It is also unlikely that witches in medieval times, most of whom were female, performed these kinds of spells—mainly because few women of this era could read. According to Davies, "Examples of women owning or using grimoires is scant before the sixteenth century" because of "the high level of female illiteracy, and the physical and social restrictions on women's access to books"[35] prior to that time. But examples do exist. Davies cites a 1499 case of a woman who gained access to a manuscript belonging to some friars. She apparently read the book several times over the course of six months and then used it to conjure demons and perform love spells.

Books of spells and incantations are not the only way the power and rituals of magic have been passed from one generation to the next. That also has been done by word of mouth. But, according to contemporary witches, only the rituals and traditions that work would have been shared and passed along to the next generations. Or, as Wiccans Misti Anslin Delaney and Wayland Raven say, "[Witches] used magick because magick worked, Gram taught Mom, who taught daughter, who taught granddaughter."[36] But whether this magic really worked cannot be determined. All that experts can say for sure is that spells have existed for millennia, real people have used magic throughout that time, and folklore and mythology have promoted the idea that magic can work.

Chapter 4

If It's Not Witchcraft, What Might It Be?

"Any sufficiently advanced technology is indistinguishable from magic."

—Science-fiction writer Arthur C. Clarke.
Quoted in Andrew Zimmerman Jones, "What Are Clarke's Laws?," About.com. http://physics.about.com.

"Magic is not science, it is a collection of ways to do things— ways that work but often we don't know why."

—Science-fiction writer Robert A. Heinlein.
Robert A. Heinlein, *Glory Road.* New York: Orb, 2006, p. 183.

When the first witch trials began in colonial Massachusetts in 1692, almost no one doubted the existence of witches and witchcraft. Witches were considered agents of the devil, and the appearance of then-unexplainable medical conditions were often taken as signs that the sufferers were victims of an evil spell or demon possession. Therefore, after nine girls in Salem Village began exhibiting bizarre symptoms, town leaders easily accepted a doctor's suggestion that the girls had been bewitched. Their symptoms included convulsions, hallucinations, body contortions, ranting, and feeling as though they were being pricked with pins and needles or pinched. The doctor's diagnosis seemed especially believable because soon after the strange behaviors started, the girls began making accusations of witchcraft.

When the trials finally came to an end in 1693, twenty people had been executed as witches. By this time, learned and respected men had cast doubt on the evidence used to gain convictions. Once this evidence was disallowed, the guilty verdicts ceased. Nonetheless, people continued to believe that witchcraft had been responsible for at least some of the girls' bizarre behaviors, and there was no way to prove whether this had indeed been the case.

Seeking Explanations

Centuries later, during the 1970s, curious researchers returned to the scene of the witch trials in hopes of uncovering other possible reasons for the strange behaviors and damaging accusations that culminated in the Salem witch scare. Many researchers operated under the theory that a physical illness was to blame. Some theorized that the symptoms were caused by the ingestion of ergot, a fungus that poisons rye. People who eat the moldy rye would likely exhibit the same types of symptoms that were seen in the girls, such as convulsions and odd skin sensations. According to records of the time, rye bread was common in the Salem area, so it is very likely that it was part of the diet of the girls whose accusations prompted the trials. It is also likely that the rye had been harvested in damp weather, which helps the fungus grow.

Other explanations have also been offered. One is that the girls ingested jimsonweed, which grows wild around Salem and also causes convulsions. Since the girls often spent time alone together outside, they might have picked and eaten the weed when others did not. Another theory is that, while they were out walking together, the girls were bitten by ticks that carry Lyme disease. In its advanced stages, this bacterial infection can cause shooting pains, numbness or tingling, and cognitive difficulties.

Lying

These and other explanations related to physical illnesses are plausible but not entirely convincing. For instance, if rye poisoning was the source of the strange behaviors, why did other townspeople not exhibit the same symptoms? Presumably everyone in the area ate the same type of bread. The simplest explanation for what prompted the Salem witch trials is that the girls were lying. The behavioral psychologist who first suggested ergot poisoning as the cause, Linnda Caporael, acknowledges that at least some of the girls lied. She reports,

> At the end of June and the beginning of July, 1692, I think there was more imagination than ergot. But by that point in time three people had already been hung, and the trials had taken a path that people felt they had to stay on. One of the clearest examples is the young accuser who, in the late summer, said "wait a minute, I don't think that there are witches after all." At that point, the other girls began accusing HER of being a witch, and she immediately seemed to understand what was going on and began being a vociferous accuser again.[37]

A lithograph shows a young girl supposedly experiencing demonic possession during the trial of a witch in Salem. The testimony of nine girls led to the trial and execution of twenty inhabitants of the town. Many modern historians believe the girls' accusations were lies to gain power and attention.

Some or all of the girls might have had other reasons to lie as well. They might have faked their symptoms and targeted particular people in hopes of pleasing their parents. It turns out that all of the people the girls accused were members of a different political faction than the girls' family members, and the enmity between the two groups was strong. Or they might simply have enjoyed the importance, power, and attention that being both victims and accusers gave them, since their social status as young girls made them unimportant, powerless, and easy to overlook.

Indeed, historians can point to other cases where witnesses lied to gain attention. This appears to have been the case, for example, during the late seventeenth century in Sweden, when mass witch trials resulted in the execution of hundreds of men and women. Many of the witnesses were children who made up elaborate stories about witches consorting with the devil. In one town, over five hundred children testified against about sixty accused witches. However, some of the stories were so outlandish that a few boys were flogged for lying. Five years later, after a convicted witch was burned alive, children began confessing their dishonesty out of guilt for what they had done. Eventually a government commission decreed that four boys who had been responsible for a particularly large number of false accusations should be put to death, thereby ending the Swedish witch craze.

Conversion Disorder

A desire for attention can also fuel cases of conversion disorder, a psychological condition more commonly known as mass hysteria. Experts believe that this disorder was at least partly, if not wholly, to blame for the Salem girls' accusations. This belief is based on the way the accusations spread: as more girls heard about the accusations, more girls developed the symptoms of apparent bewitchment, and they in turn began participating in the accusation of others. Specifically, the symptoms started with two girls who lived in the same house, nine-year-old Elizabeth "Betty" Parris and eleven-year-old Abigail Williams, but they quickly spread to the other girls in their group of friends.

When symptoms spread from one person to another, despite the absence of a contagious disease, psychologists might suspect

Were Witches on Drugs?

In centuries past, when people confessed to practicing witchcraft, they described activities like flying on broomsticks, dancing with wild abandon, and seeing strange things. Upon hearing these stories, modern-day medical experts have noted that such experiences could be the product of drug use. Indeed, one sixteenth-century physician wrote of a witch having an ointment made of herbs that included hemlock, nightshade, henbane, and mandrake. These contain chemicals called tropane alkaloids, which can cause hallucinations. In fact, one of these chemicals, scopolamine (an active ingredient in some travel-sickness medicines), can create an altered state of consciousness when used in high doses. Moreover, physicians say that an easy way to transmit the chemical into the body is via the skin—which would occur if a witch rubbed the ointment on her body in significant amounts.

that a conversion disorder is at work. This disorder fits with the symptoms displayed by the girls. It also happens to be especially common among teenagers, particularly girls. Experts say that girls who long for attention are more prone to develop conversion disorder. As Jane Mendle, a clinical psychologist and assistant professor at Cornell University who specializes in treating adolescent girls, reports,

> One of the things that is most noticeable about conversion disorder is that it tends to occur in people who don't necessarily command a lot of social attention; by social attention, I really mean society's attention—in that they are not the focus of their society. And historically and traditionally that's women. So when you look to things like the Salem Witch Trials, these girls were by no means a focus of their community until they developed their

physical symptoms. And then they became a center of a town's narrative in a way they would have never have been able to otherwise.[38]

Cultural Influences

But while conversion disorder might explain why the girls exhibited the symptoms of the bewitched, it does not explain why the people of Salem were so eager to believe that they had succumbed to witchcraft. Cultural influences provide one explanation. As authors Garvin McCain and Erwin Segal point out, "For us, it is almost impossible to believe in witches; for our ancestors, it was equally difficult to deny their existence. Our new beliefs exist, in part, due to the development of 'scientific attitudes.'"[39]

Indeed, Salem in the 1600s was under the influence of the same factors that led to the executions of hundreds of thousands of suspected witches in Europe between the fifteenth and seventeenth centuries. The people of both time periods had a strong belief in magic, a fear of the unknown, a great deal of ignorance about the workings of the human body and mind, and the widespread conviction that one's misfortunes could be caused by the devil. Had they lived in a culture in which medicine, psychology, and other sciences held sway, the people of Salem might not have been drawn so quickly to witchcraft as the cause of the strange behaviors. Instead, they might have looked for a scientific explanation for the girls' problems.

Hysteria like that displayed in Salem can occur in modern times as well. In Le Roy, New York, in 2012, for example, teenagers began exhibiting symptoms that included fainting, involuntary twitching, and clapping. The first person to display these symptoms was sixteen-year-old Lori Brownell. As other teens heard about or saw her symptoms, some of them developed them, too. Experts there first ruled out physical causes, including exposure to an unknown

> "For us, it is almost impossible to believe in witches; for our ancestors, it was equally difficult to deny their existence. Our new beliefs exist, in part, due to the development of 'scientific attitudes.'"[39]
>
> —Garvin McCain and Erwin Segal in their 1969 book The Game of Science.

toxin, and then moved on to psychological ones. They concluded that the victims—thirteen girls and one boy—were experiencing conversion disorder.

Religious Climate

Knowledge also plays a role in assumptions regarding witchcraft. The people of colonial Massachusetts were unaware of conversion disorder. They also knew of only one ailment that could cause some of the symptoms that the girls were experiencing: epilepsy. Once epilepsy was ruled out, the evidence seemed to point in only one direction: witchcraft. This evidence included the girls' physical symptoms; the insistence by a physician who had examined the girls, Dr. William Griggs of Salem Village, that their afflictions were caused by an evil entity rather than natural causes; and the fact that the girls had been dabbling in witchcraft with a family slave, Tituba, prior to the appearance of their symptoms.

Epilepsy can cause involuntary spasms similar to those exhibited by the girls who claimed to be possessed during the Salem witch trials of 1692–93. However, colonial physicians were familiar with cases of epilepsy and ruled that illness out, leaving many to conclude that witchcraft was to blame.

The religious climate of the community would also have contributed to the villagers' reactions. During the 1600s, Salem was made up mostly of Puritans, a type of English Protestant with strict moral beliefs. Their religion taught that witchcraft was evil and not to be tolerated—a fact that would have made the girls fearful and anxious about the possibility that they might get caught practicing it. This fear and anxiety, psychiatrists note, would have made them more vulnerable to conversion disorder.

In colonial times, Puritans also viewed religion as being important to all aspects of life. As forensic psychiatrist Susan Hatters Friedman and mental health expert Andrew Howie explain, "God and the Devil were in daily contact with the colonists. The Puritan church was the center of the community, spiritually and politically." Therefore, they say, "attempts to understand Salem require that we shed our 21st century worldview and imagine the context of 1692 Salem . . . [where] separation of fantasy from reality was quite different from today, and a belief in witchcraft was part of the culture."[40]

> "Attempts to understand Salem require that we shed our 21st century worldview and imagine the context of 1692 Salem . . . [where] separation of fantasy from reality was quite different from today, and a belief in witchcraft was part of the culture."[40]
>
> —Forensic psychiatrist Susan Hatters Friedman and mental health expert Andrew Howie.

Nonetheless, a few people did challenge the notion that witchcraft—or at least witchcraft as it had been presented via witch trials in America and Europe—was real. One such person was Thomas Ady. In his 1656 book, *A Candle in the Dark*, Ady suggested that witch hunts were attempts by the church "to delude the people"[41] into thinking that religious devotion would protect them from things like illnesses and storms.

But Ady and a few others like him could not overcome the view that the widespread belief in witches meant they *had* to be real. This was the argument in the 1668 book *Of Credulity and Incredulity* by theologian Meric Casaubon. Scientist Carl Sagan discusses Casaubon's views in his own book, *The Demon-Haunted World*. Casaubon's argument, Sagan explains, is "that witches must exist because, after all, everyone believes in them. Anything that a large number of people believe must be true."[42]

Sagan notes that the advent of modern science did much to dispel this attitude:

> For much of our history, we were so fearful of the outside world, with its unpredictable dangers, that we gladly embraced anything that promised to soften or explain away the terror. Science is an attempt, largely successful, to understand the world, to get a grip on things, to get hold of ourselves, to steer a safe course. Microbiology and meteorology now explain what only a few centuries ago was considered sufficient cause to burn women to death.[43]

The Difficulties of Proof

Without such explanations, people must accept things based on faith. But in a culture that embraces science, this can be difficult to do. Many people say that if supernatural forces like witchcraft are real, there must be proof to support this. But because magic is an invisible force—if indeed it exists—there is no way to prove that it actually causes things to happen. A person's job promotion, for example, could be due to a magic spell for good fortune cast by a witch the previous day. But it could also be due to hard work, a generous boss, or someone else quitting and leaving the position open. And when a witch casts a spell to heal someone and that person's illness subsequently goes away, there is no way to know whether there was a cause-and-effect relationship between the spell and the healing since bodies sometimes heal with time and treatment.

Sagan equates this kind of situation to one where someone claims to have an invisible dragon in his garage. Upon hearing this claim, an objective person would propose various ways to test it. One could, for example, try to spray-paint the dragon to make it show up or dust the floor with flour so that the creature's footprints would be visible. But if the claimant rejected these suggestions, providing a variety of excuses that included the idea that none would work when conducted by a doubter, the objective person would likely become a skeptic.

Moreover, even if several other people also claimed to have dragons in their garages, and one of them held up a burnt finger

Using Science to Create Magic

Queen Elizabeth I of England appointed mathematician, astronomer, astrologer, and occultist John Dee to be the royal adviser on mystic secrets. This allowed Dee to conduct scientific studies on various magical arts under royal protection, even though others would have been arrested for doing so. His main focuses were divination and alchemy, although he also studied other forms of magic and sought to communicate with angels. A forerunner of chemistry, alchemy involved laboratory attempts to convert one form of matter into another. The conversion most often associated with alchemy is turning base metals into gold, but alchemists also sought to create an elixir that would cure all diseases. Mastering alchemy was also believed to be a stepping stone to great magical powers, including immortality.

saying his dragon had breathed invisible fire on it, the skeptic would not take this as proof that invisible dragons are real. As Sagan explains,

> We understand that there are other ways to burn fingers besides the breath of invisible dragons. Such "evidence"—no matter how important the dragon advocates consider it—is far from compelling . . . [and] the only sensible approach is tentatively to reject the dragon hypothesis, to be open to future physical data, and to wonder what the cause might be that so many apparently sane and sober people share the same strange delusion.[44]

Thoughts and Reality

Science, many people hope, will one day be able to prove that magic is real. "What seems like magic today," says author and witch William H. Keith, "may well be the hard science of tomorrow."[45] In fact, some witches think that quantum physics, which concerns how matter and energy behave at microscopic levels, offers great promise in this regard.

According to physicists, when researchers observe photons—the tiny packets of energy that light is made of—they might view the photons as either a series of specks or a string-like wave. Studies have shown that whether a photon appears one way or the other depends on what the observer expects to see. In other words, belief seems to affect the nature of a photon—though not all scientists believe that this is actually the case. Many witches view this apparent finding as confirmation of their conviction that thoughts can influence the natural world.

As further proof that thoughts can affect reality, witches point to their widely held conviction that a spell will work only if the people present during the casting of that spell believe it will work. For this reason, witches say, whenever a skeptic observes witchcraft, that witchcraft is doomed to fail. Beliefs strongly influence what a person sees and what that person acknowledges to be real. But skeptics counter that if magic were real then spells would work in the presence of believers, nonbelievers, and neutral parties alike.

> "What seems like magic today may well be the hard science of tomorrow."[45]
>
> —Witch William H. Keith in his book The Science of the Craft.

Subconscious Minds

From the point of view of skeptics, many events attributed to magic can actually be explained as coincidences. But could coincidences be evidence of magic at work? Psychiatrist Carl Jung (1875–1961) thought that the subconscious mind could produce what he called significant coincidences, or synchronicity.

An example of synchronicity concerns a man who was treated to some plum pudding by a stranger at a restaurant. Ten years later he ordered plum pudding again at a different restaurant but was told by the waiter that another customer had gotten the last of it—the same stranger who had treated the man to plum pudding years earlier. Years later the man who had lost his pudding

Followers of religion or those who believe in witchcraft share a devoted faith in mystical powers. The similarity extends to the use of icons and totems, the enactment of rituals, the speaking of sacred words, and the collecting and sharing of lore and spiritual wisdom.

to the stranger told friends this story over dinner—whereupon the stranger walked into the room. Such coincidences, Jung concluded, were too improbable to be considered random.

Moreover, Jung suspected that synchronicity was responsible for photons and other quantum entities changing their state depending on the observer. He felt that the subconscious mind—or a collection of subconscious minds, which he called the collective unconscious—was somehow influencing events. In discussing this theory, some people say that it is why they believe that tarot cards can predict future events. Specifically, the subconscious mind of the tarot card reader focuses on the cards to determine what they mean. Once this meaning is seen—as with the photons affected by the observer—the future predicted in the cards is likely to become the reality.

Total Belief

However, theories related to how the mind might influence magic are speculation. They have not been proven and must therefore be taken on faith, just as with religious beliefs. Interestingly, scholars have long considered magic to be akin to religion. French sociologist Marcel Mauss (1872–1950), for example, noted that although religion and witchcraft have different ends—religion offers intangible rewards, and magic is intended to bring tangible results—there are many similarities between the two. Both use rites and sacred objects to encourage belief, involve supernatural powers and traditions, and require total belief from their followers.

Others have noted that both magic and religion have important roles in society. Both provide believers with explanations for the unexplainable and give them hope that their efforts (whether magical or prayerful) will improve their lives. In addition, both witches and the religious faithful generally do not care if others think their beliefs foolish. Nor do they care about the absence of scientific evidence to explain the magical or miraculous; they remain certain that such things exist.

Source Notes

Introduction: Witches and Witchcraft

1. Patti Wigington, "Can I Be a Christian Wiccan or Witch?," About Religion. http://paganwiccan.about.com.

2. Zöe Grace, "Can You Be a Christian Witch?," Zöe's Magickal Garden. http://witchychristian.tripod.com.

3. Quoted in Vincent M. Mallozzi, "Lessons in Modern Witchcraft, Minus the Broomsticks," *City Room* (blog), *New York Times*, June 16, 2013. http://cityroom.blogs.nytimes.com.

4. Quoted in Mallozzi, "Lessons in Modern Witchcraft, Minus the Broomsticks."

Chapter One: What Is Witchcraft?

5. Estelle Daniels, "Ceremonial Magick and the Average Person," 2003. www.estelledaniels.com.

6. Sarah Anne Lawless, "Pantry Folk Magic," August 1, 2013. http://sarahannelawless.com.

7. Joseph Glanvill, *Saducismus Triumphatus; or, Full and Plain Evidence Concerning Witches and Apparitions,* 3rd ed. London Printed for S. Lownds at his Shoppe by the Savoy-Gate, 1688. http://ebooks.library.cornell.edu.

8. Glanvill, *Saducismus Triumphatus,* p. 109.

9. Lynn Windsor, "Where Does Magic Come From?," Pagan Pages, January 2, 2008. http://pagan-pages.org.

10. Quoted in Niels Ebdrup, "Your Danish Friend May Be a Witch," Science Nordic, June 4, 2012. http://sciencenordic.com.

11. Quoted in Ebdrup, "Your Danish Friend May Be a Witch."

12. Paul Dale Roberts, "Interview with a Witch: The Donna Reynolds Story," Fire Ring. www.thefirering.com.

Chapter Two: Why Do People Believe in Witchcraft?

13. Quoted in Natalie Wolchover, "Why Everyone Believes in Magic (Even You)," LiveScience, April 12, 2012. www.livescience.com.

14. Quoted in Wolchover, "Why Everyone Believes in Magic (Even You)."

15. Wolchover, "Why Everyone Believes in Magic (Even You)."

16. Quoted in Lauren Mackay, "How and Why Did the Ancient Greeks Employ Magic?," History Files, February 11, 2011. www.thehistoryfiles.com.

17. Quoted in DeliriumsRealm, "Heresy, Magic, and Witchcraft in Early Modern Europe." www.deliriumsrealm.com.

18. Quoted in Hanover College History Department, "Reginald Scot, 'The Discovery of Witchcraft' (London, 1584)," ed. Frank Luttmer. http://history.hanover.edu.

19. Quoted in Gustav Henningsen, ed., *The Salazar Documents: Inquisitor Alonso de Salazar Frías and Others on the Basque Persecution*, Google Books, p. 93. https://books.google.com.

20. James Hannam, "The Decline and End of Witch Trials in Europe," Bede's Library, April 10, 2003. www.bede.org.uk.

21. Hannam, "The Decline and End of Witch Trials in Europe."

22. Wolchover, "Why Everyone Believes in Magic (Even You)."

23. Quoted in David E. Miller, "Saudi Arabia's 'Anti-witchcraft Unit' Breaks Another Spell," *Jerusalem Post*, July 20, 2011. www.jpost.com.

24. Quoted in Softpedia, "Why Do We Believe in Witchcraft and Magic?," October 25, 2007. http://archive.news.softpedia .com.

Chapter Three: Is Witchcraft More Myth than Magic?

25. Faust.com, "Witchcraft," 2010. www.faust.com.

26. Faust.com, "Witchcraft."

27. Angela Sangster, "The Witch—Origins Myths & Truths About Witchcraft & Witches," True Ghost Tales, 2010. www.true ghosttales.com.

28. Sangster, "The Witch."

29. Quoted in Rachel Bletchly, "How to Spot a Witch: Believers' Methods from the 15th to the 18th Centuries," *Mirror,* October 31, 2014. www.mirror.co.uk.

30. Quoted in *The Creation of Anne Boleyn* (blog)*,* "The Anne Boleyn Mythbuster: #1 Anne's Looks," October 3, 2011. https://thecreationofanneboleyn.wordpress.com.

31. Faust.com, "Witchcraft."

32. Witchcraft, "Egyptian Witchcraft." www.witchcraft.com.au.

33. Quoted in Margot Adler, *Drawing Down the Moon: Witches, Druids, Goddess-Worshippers, and Other Pagans in America Today.* Boston: Beacon, 2005, p. 173.

34. Owen Davies, *Grimoires: A History of Magic Books.* Oxford, UK: Oxford University Press, 2009, page 1.

35. Davies, *Grimoires,* pp. 41–42.

36. Misti Anslin Delaney and Wayland Raven, "A Not-So-Broken Tradition," Beliefnet. www.beliefnet.com.

Chapter Four: If It's Not Witchcraft, What Might It Be?

37. *Secrets of the Undead*, "The Witches Curse: Behavioral Psychologist Linnda Caporael Interview," PBS. www.pbs.org.

38. Quoted in Hayley Krischer, "Hysteria and Teenage Girls," Hairpin, March 13, 2015. http://thehairpin.com.

39. Quoted in Richard Olson, "Spirits, Witches & Science: Why the Rise of Science Encouraged Belief in the Supernatural in 17th-Century England," *Skeptic*, 1992.

40. Susan Hatters Friedman and Andrew Howie, "Salem Witchcraft and Lessons for Contemporary Forensics Psychiatry," *Journal of the American Academy of Psychiatry and the Law*, June 2013. www.jaapl.org.

41. Quoted in Carl Sagan, *The Demon-Haunted World: Science as "A Candle in the Dark."* New York: Ballantine, 1996, p. 26.

42. Sagan, *The Demon-Haunted World,* p. 117.

43. Sagan, *The Demon-Haunted World,* p. 26.

44. Sagan, *The Demon-Haunted World,* p. 173.

45. William H. Keith, *The Science of the Craft: Modern Realities in the Ancient Art of Witchcraft.* New York: Citadel, 2005, p. 60.

For Further Research

Books

Skye Alexander, *The Modern Guide to Witchcraft: Your Complete Guide to Witches, Covens, and Spells.* Avon, MA: Adams Media, 2014.

Richard Godbeer, *The Salem Witch Hunt: A Brief History with Documents*. Boston: Bedford/St. Martin's, 2011.

Michael Howard, *Modern Wicca: A History from Gerald Gardner to the Present.* Woodbury, MN: Llewellyn, 2010.

Katherine Howe, *The Penguin Book of Witches.* New York: Penguin Classics, 2014.

Christine Hoff Kraemer, *Seeking the Mystery: An Introduction to Pagan Theologies.* Englewood, CO: Patheos, 2012.

Richard Marshall, *Witchcraft: Ancient Origins to the Present Day*. Glasgow, Scotland: Saraband, 2012.

Patricia D. Netzley, *The Greenhaven Encyclopedia of Witchcraft*. San Diego: Greenhaven, 2002.

Internet Sources

Erik Davis, "A Skeptic's Guide to Magical Thinking," Skeptic North. www.skepticnorth.com/2010/10/a-skeptics-guide-to-magical-thinking-part-1.

Encyclopedia of Occultism and Parapsychology, "Witchcraft," Encyclopedia.com. www.encyclopedia.com/topic/witchcraft.aspx.

Sam Harris, "In Defense of Witchcraft," *Huffington Post*, May 25, 2011. www.huffingtonpost.com/sam-harris/in-defense-of-witch craft_b_53865.html.

Witchcraft: A Guide to the Misunderstood and the Maligned, "What Is Witchcraft." www.witchcraftandwitches.com/index.html.

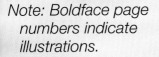

Index

Picture Credits

Cover: Thinkstock Images

Associated Press: 49

Depositphotos: 34

ermess/Shutterstock.com: 23

© John Harper/Corbis: 67

© Heritage Images/Corbis: 53

Alisdair Macdonald/REX/Newscom: 16

National Library of Medicine/Science Photo Library: 62

rook76/Shutterstock.com: 45

© George Steinmetz/Corbis: 41

Thinkstock Images: 14

© Trolley Dodger/Corbis: 8

Magic spells from the Book of the Dead, papyrus, detail/De Agostini Picture Library/A. Dagli Orti/Bridgeman Images: 30

Witches of Salem – a girl bewitched at a trial in 1692 (color litho), American School/Private Collection/Peter Newark American Pictures/Bridgeman Images: 58

About the
Author

Patricia D. Netzley is the author of dozens of books for children, teens, and adults. She writes both fiction and nonfic-
tion and is a member of the Society of Children's Book Writ-
ers and Illustrators.